# THE PERFECT KITCHEN

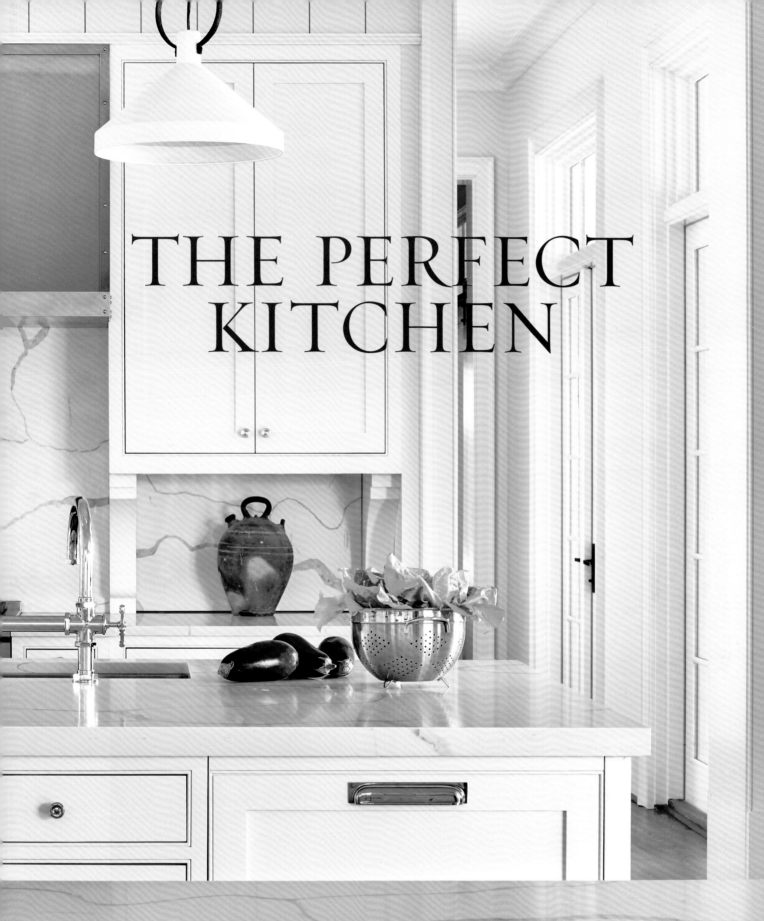

# THE PERFECT KITCHEN

## BARBARA SALLICK

### WRITTEN WITH MARC KRISTAL

For
Peter Sallick

---

. . . and my Waterworks
colleagues and friends,
past and present

# Contents

# Introduction

A few years back, a highly regarded and very talented New York architect was engaged to design a dream home for a wealthy client on the South Shore of Long Island. This man had the means to fulfill his most elaborate fantasies, and with his architect's aid, he did—in spades. The outcome, which drew on Shingle Style precedents by Charles McKim, Stanford White, and other legendary practitioners, rambled for thousands of square feet in every direction, spanning game rooms, libraries, parlors, salons, porches, dining halls, and countless bedrooms supported by sitting areas, dressing rooms, and baths.

The architect, who had managed to pull off this programmatic feat with elegance and restraint, was justifiably proud of what he'd accomplished. But when asked which of the many rooms his client preferred above all the others, he sighed philosophically. "Mostly the guy hangs out in the kitchen," he said, "like the rest of us."

This story reminds us that we've come full circle in recent years. The original room, as it were, *was* the kitchen: back in the Stone Age, you had a cave with a fire on which you prepared your bronto burgers, and that was pretty much it. In the thousands of years since, residences have gotten bigger, rooms have been added, and functions have multiplied beyond our wildest imaginings. Yet despite the many millennia of progress, like latter-day Flintstones, we've gravitated back to that essential space—and to the idea of the kitchen as home.

The role of the kitchen has certainly evolved over time. In the great homes of the late nineteenth and early twentieth centuries, the room was almost completely disconnected from a residence's public spaces and seldom part of the larger decorative environment. Tellingly, when you look through books featuring the work of great prewar decorators like Dorothy Draper and Frances Elkins, the kitchens aren't featured. Why would anyone who aspired to a gracious style of living want to look at a lot of sinks and stoves?

Today, by contrast, architects and designers spend a great deal of time adding enough square footage to accommodate kitchens, breakfast rooms, and dens—the holy trinity of modern living—when renovating classic homes. They also explicitly connect these rooms to more formal spaces, which are typically reserved for special occasions.

The balance began to shift in the 1950s and '60s, with the suburban kitchen becoming more of a family hub, especially around mealtimes. But kitchens back then weren't *planned*—people (i.e., women) thought nothing of walking across the room from the sink to put a plate in the dishwasher, usually beneath a single glaring overhead light. While postwar innovations like electric can openers and Mixmasters celebrated efficiency, words like *flow* and *functionality* hadn't yet entered the homemaker's vocabulary. As for the idea of actually *decorating* or designing a kitchen, forget it. If you had linoleum on the floor, Formica on the countertops, and shelf paper in the cabinets, your kitchen reigned as the height of chic. (No one had islands, either—an island was where Gilligan got stuck.)

Four things, in my view, have led to the kitchen's change of fortune. The first is that domestic life is at once more informal and more child-centered—the wants and needs of a family's youngest members have moved to the forefront. Inevitably, kids go where the food is: they are always hungry, prefer that mealtime be a virtually 24/7 affair, and pursue a myriad of tasks and pleasures at the kitchen table. And where children go, parents follow. More and more, in an age in which people rarely venture into formal public rooms, the destination is the kitchen.

Another powerful contributor to the rise of the kitchen is the explosion of interest in all things food-related. Every major newspaper today has a culinary section, the internet overflows with recipes, food networks proliferate, and whereas fifty years ago there was only the formidable figure of Julia Child exhorting us to "Save the liver!" celebrity chefs are now as ubiquitous as chain drugstores. And when we see Ina, Martha, Wolfgang, Rachael, Gordon, Jamie, Lidia, or Emeril, they're naturally in the kitchen, showing us not only how to prepare the perfect dish, but also how to appoint a space for maximum effectiveness and, not least, aesthetic pleasure.

That emphasis on looks suggests the third reason that the kitchen has become the heart of the home: a booming interest in design. I've experienced this personally. When Waterworks opened its doors four decades ago, almost no one thought about the bathroom in terms of style. Today, that's changed: design has become a cornerstone of American culture and is constantly improving the way life is lived, even in private spaces. Given the rising prominence of the kitchen and our propensity to spend ever more time there, it was perhaps inevitable that the room's desirability and decor would become one. Draper and Elkins might not have published their kitchens, but rare is the interior design book that excludes them today.

The fourth factor underlying the kitchen's increasing prominence is one that influences every aspect of modern life: technology. There was a time not so very long ago when homes actually contained small spaces called telephone rooms, into which people would retreat to make calls. Now, *every* room is the telephone room—and the media room, the office, and the game room. If whatever you want to do can follow you wherever you want to go, the last obstacle standing between you and the kitchen has been removed for good.

Though Waterworks, the bath company that my husband, Robert, and I began in the 1970s, has always created fixtures and finishes for the kitchen, we've recently intensified our focus on this

This early twentieth-century room points to an enduring truism about kitchens: whether bare bones or well-equipped, utilitarian or elaborately decorated, they remain the inviting, consoling heart of the home.

special space. Back when we first began thinking critically about the bath, we realized that style and functionality had to go hand in hand: the task was to improve, refine, and expand upon both aspects simultaneously. We also discovered that Waterworks did best when we went both backward and forward at the same time, by reintroducing and reinventing Edwardian-style bath fixtures so that they felt at once familiar and new.

Applied to the kitchen, this particular paradigm gets you only so far. For one, a bathroom has four unchanging elements: a sink, a shower, a tub, and a water closet. A kitchen, by contrast, is a vastly more complicated affair with an array of appliances (movable and fixed), storage zones, adjacencies, and perishables. What's more, a bath is essentially a private space visited periodically throughout the course of a day. The kitchen, conversely, is a multifunctional social arena used from very early in the morning until well after sundown. As for aesthetics, Robert and I discovered that for the bath, our customers preferred all-white elements that hewed to tradition; in the kitchen, they fearlessly mixed colors, finishes, and styles.

Into this brave new world we have boldly sailed, and what follows is the outcome of our investigations: a book that looks at all aspects of kitchen design and will help you get your arms around a process of creation in which planning is paramount. For decades, I have counseled people to plan their baths with the utmost care and forethought, as the mistakes you make without doing so are not

OPPOSITE: Simply by studying the environment in which Julia Child labored, Americans learned as much from her about kitchen design as they did about cooking. RIGHT: Jack Lemmon demonstrates his backhand with a pot of spaghetti in *The Apartment*.

the sort that can be fixed with a coat of paint. When it comes to kitchens, planning is exponentially more critical, and the price one pays (existentially as well as financially) for not being diligent is infinitely higher. Though most of us don't think of it as such, the kitchen is by far the most complex room in the home. Getting everything organized prior to installation is the key to achieving an efficient renovation and a timeless, high-functioning space. *The Perfect Kitchen* is a comprehensive guide to the task.

In Billy Wilder's 1960 film *The Apartment*, there is a wonderfully funny moment in which Jack Lemmon—laboring in the sort of cramped and grubby New York kitchen that would give a cockroach pause—drains a pot of spaghetti using a tennis racket. The scene's charm derives from the fact that he clearly has a good time doing it, and therein lies the key to a truly successful kitchen: the quality of the experience. For all of the practical questions one needs to ask about storage, equipment, ventilation, gas and water lines, and finishes, the most important one is this: what kind of experience do I want to create?

I love my kitchen. I'd give myself a B as a cook, but that's not the point (unless you're a dinner guest, though my scampi seldom disappoints). What I really enjoy is the process of getting everything in place—leafing through the recipe book on the countertop, opening the cabinets and drawers, pulling out the right pots and utensils, laying out the ingredients. To me, the pleasure lies in these thoughtful steps, which are part of my gift to the people for whom I cook. I also love the process because my kitchen is specifically designed to simplify and enhance it.

Of course, everyone has his or her own idea of the perfect kitchen experience, even if it's opening up a takeout container. It is my hope that *The Perfect Kitchen* will make it easy—and even fun—to get there, in a space that's thoroughly your own.

13

PART I

# Matters of Style

As the heart of the home, the kitchen touches on realms of memory and intimacy—elements much more challenging to get right than functionality or flow. How the room looks determines how it makes you feel, which is why, in the kitchen, finding the right style remains essential.

# Style, Defined

In the following chapter, I will explore the critical issue of functionality and present a linear process designed to ensure that your kitchen answers all of your practical needs. But before we talk about how your kitchen *works*, let us first think about how you want this most crucial of spaces to *look*. I know that seems counterintuitive: surely, getting the flow of your kitchen right takes precedence over matters of style? In fact, the opposite is the case. Once you have crystallized your needs and a kitchen consultant has thoughtfully translated them into a program, that challenge has largely been met. But kitchen style is trickier. It goes beyond modern versus traditional, or even how to create a room that aligns aesthetically with the rest of your home (a matter easily resolved by your architect or decorator). As the heart of your home, the kitchen touches on realms of memory and intimacy, elements much more challenging to get right than hardware or paint color.

What do we mean, *really*, when we talk about style? Let me respond by making a mildly controversial confession: even though functionality remains of the utmost importance, I would be willing to compromise on it a bit, if doing so meant that I got a kitchen that looked and, more to the point, *felt* the way I require. Yes, your kitchen needs to be a model of efficiency, and if you invest a great deal of time and money and end up with something that doesn't work the way you expected, you will be desolate. But—and here is my point—if your kitchen doesn't *look* right, you will be every bit as disappointed and probably even more so. That is because, as noted in the introduction to this book, the kitchen is everyone's favorite gathering spot, the room that you and your family visit again and again in the course of every day. And because you are in there so frequently, and for reasons that are as much about consolation, nurturing, and reassurance as more quotidian matters of function, your kitchen has to hit its mark, visually, aesthetically, *emotionally*, 100 percent of the time.

There's a hilarious scene in the TV series *The Marvelous Mrs. Maisel* in which the heroine, a '50s-era housewife, gets up early to do her hair and makeup (false lashes included), then slips back into bed and pretends to wake up again, so her husband only ever sees her looking perfect. It's a throwback idea that's surprisingly relevant to today's kitchen: the room should meet your expectations every time you lay eyes on it.

How do you widen a narrow pantry—this one, which sits behind the kitchen on the pages that follow—and keep it stylish? With narrow shelves precisely customized to fit their contents and white and transparent elements that don't feel oppressive.

What is surprising about this kitchen is that it is clean-lined and modern without being anonymous or impersonal; elements such as the rectilinear tiled backsplash provide texture and character. I also appreciate how the simplicity of this small space enables it to cohabit comfortably with its surroundings.

# Keeping It Personal

How *does* one begin to think personally about the kitchen and then translate that into a design? The key lies in picturing it as a room that you have a relationship with and imagining what that emotional experience should be like—that, to my mind, is the essence of successful kitchen design. When pondering how you want your kitchen to look, you should absolutely refer to the tear sheets and books and online image banks that you've been saving. But no less important is thinking about all the kitchens in which you've had memorable experiences and examining those memories closely. Look at it this way: if you were designing the perfect beach house, you'd first think experientially rather than aesthetically, going back in your mind to all the great waterfront getaways you've visited. Was there a view, a veranda with curtains that fluttered in the ocean breeze, a chair that reclined at just the right angle? All of these components would come to mind precisely because you'd want to create a dependably enjoyable experience. And your kitchen—the room in which you and your family and friends spend so much time, your home's default comfort zone—is no different. How it looks is tightly bound up with what you like to do in it—or think you might enjoy doing in the future—and how these activities make you *feel*.

So give yourself the time and the permission to fantasize about the kitchen experiences that would give you maximum comfort and enjoyment. Perhaps it's brewing a perfect cup of coffee and sitting quietly with it at a table washed by the morning light. Or gathering with family members who help you prepare a sumptuous holiday dinner. Or perhaps you've always wanted to have your cookbooks on a shelf at eye level above your prep area, rather than in a cupboard, so you can immediately survey your options.

However you choose to design your kitchen, it's useful to remember that every component—including the food itself and how you arrange and display it—is part of an overall experience combining aesthetics, utility, and, not least, taste.

The austere elegance of this kitchen—its simple, symmetrical architectural elements, careful alignment of marble countertops, and rich blue lacquerwork— is softened by the curvaceous profile of the barstools and inviting window seat.

While this kitchen might appear to be a random cornucopia at a glance, certain elements suggest a distinct narrative character: the Emeco stools, the laboratory pendant light, the schoolroom clock, and, not least, the chunky vintage TV. I see a cafeteria in a scientific research facility, circa 1980. Not everyone would, but that invitation to interpret gives this kitchen character.

This classical kitchen, with its traditional checkerboard floor, crown moldings, and sleek materiality, embraces both the luxury of space and amenities and the simplicity of the homespun.

ABOVE AND OPPOSITE: The components of this country kitchen—actually overlooking a body of water in Nova Scotia—conspire to capture a spirit of culinary collaboration, casualness, and comfort. Little is concealed, surfaces are user-friendly, and seating is inviting and abundant. Such an environment makes room for everything—even the vintage cloth shade on the hanging light.

And while you're fantasizing about the memories you're going to make, think back on the ones you've stored away. Many of the kitchens you remember most warmly probably weren't perfect in the conventional sense. My grandmother's kitchen, to cite a favorite example, wasn't what you'd call cutting-edge. But I recall with special poignancy the enormous porcelain sink and sitting around her table. By contemporary standards, my grandmother's kitchen was filled with flaws, but it had personality and it was welcoming and hardworking. These factors lie at the core of any successful kitchen design. Combining the memories you take and the ones you make equals the *truly* perfect kitchen.

I always encourage people to think very freely about design, to seek inspiration everywhere, and, above all, to keep an open mind. A prime example of the latter can be found opposite, where you'll discover an English kitchen swathed in a charmingly patterned wallpaper. As you might imagine, we pondered a multitude of images for inclusion in this book, and though every conceivable consideration was brought to bear on our choices, no one on my team had *ever* considered wallpaper. Yet the instant we caught sight of this photo, we all agreed it had to go in. That wallpaper evokes countryside, coziness, quirkiness, and craft. I could see myself sitting in that room, tea and a scone before me, in a condition of absolute contentment. The moral: don't say no to any design idea without first taking it around the track. You never know.

The combination of a baby-blue AGA stove and a charmingly patterned wallpaper makes this English country kitchen irresistibly cozy, a mood supported by the glass-front freestanding armoire, cut-glass ceiling fixture, and the dining/work table. An important note: the comfortable dining chairs seem ready-made for long meals and sustained contemplation.

ABOVE AND OPPOSITE: This space, with its extravagant stone double sink, unfinished wide-plank floors, and open shelving, demonstrates how the traditional farm-style kitchen-and-dining room paradigm can be modernized with luxurious materials, elegant tableaux, and handsome antique furnishings.

Boards and bricks equal brawn here, and just to be sure the point is made, the pendant lights above the bunkhouse table are as rusty as buckets. Pull up a saddle-style stool and sip some Chardonnay.

ABOVE: The copper sink and its hardware have been allowed to patinate, which, in addition to relieving you of polishing duties, contributes an overlay of homespun personality. OPPOSITE: The brick floor, stacked stone wall, and lichenous lintel suggest an outdoor space that has been enclosed to create, appropriately, a flower room.

There is a rigor to this room that arises from repetition. The diamond pattern of the transparent upper cabinets reappears as opaque on the lower ones. Floor and ceiling boards, differently finished, are of approximately the same width and travel in the same direction. Cornices are identical and live at the same level. The one wild card is the extravagant William Morris–influenced frieze, which, by shaking things up, paradoxically pulls it all together.

Most of this kitchen's
elements suggest an
urbane formality—the tall,
dark, and handsome
doors in particular. Yet
this clearly is a room
equipped for serious
cooking, and the synco-
pated tile floor under-
girds the serious mood
with a dash of Mondrian-
esque boogie-woogie.

ABOVE AND OPPOSITE: Though many of us fear it, strong color can be our friend, adding an enlivening accent, tying a space together, or establishing a mood. Certain shades—in this case turquoise, lacquered to a high sheen—are particularly effective at pleasurably contravening expectations, as they represent what might be described as a fearless choice.

ABOVE AND OPPOSITE: It is a myth that industrial elements can only be deployed in high-tech settings. In both of these very different kitchens, the utilitarian speed rail supporting the tables seems not only at home, but also appropriate.

# Systems or Custom—or Both?

A great kitchen isn't about perfect performance, but rather about striking an acceptable balance between appearance and utility. In thinking about this, a useful paradigm can be found in the difference between "systems" (or "fitted") and custom kitchens. Regarding the former, there are a number of high-profile European companies that market kitchens composed of prefabricated components, typically of the highest quality and contemporary in style, that can be combined and configured according to your needs and circumstances. Custom kitchens, conversely, are as the term suggests: individually designed and crafted, typically from organic materials, by artisans or studios whose objective is to give you an experience that is soulful, unique, and exquisitely beautiful.

The strengths and shortcomings of each are as you might expect. Systems kitchens tend to be streamlined, highly efficient, minimalist, and almost clinically sleek: they feature no quirkiness and often no hardware. For a strict modernist, the aesthetic can be ideal. But for traditional—or, more typically, transitional—houses, more warmth is required, and that's where the beauty of custom kitchens shine. Sublimely made from fine raw materials, they tend to be rich in personality and reveal the hand of the artisan. Yet as with any kitchen, the functionality and ultimate success of these bespoke spaces depend largely on the skill of the experts who construct and install them.

As you can imagine, based on what I've expressed thus far, the welcoming qualities of a custom kitchen are, to me, indispensable. At the same time, I'm no different from anyone else—I want water to appear when I turn on the tap and the sink-disposal motor to start grinding away when I throw the switch. Thus, the ideal remains a hybrid of both: the quality and predictable performance of a systems kitchen matched with the warmth and uniqueness of its custom counterpart—infused with a personality that suits your own.

Most of the kitchens in these pages, you will discover, are custom designed and crafted, many of them down to the smallest detail. Yet because they were meticulously composed by architects, decorators, and kitchen consultants (sometimes all three) and executed by skilled contractors and tradespeople, they are also highly functional. I hope that the variety and imagination on display in these pages will inspire you to think, in the most personal terms, about what the perfect kitchen means to you, and to trust that you can fully achieve it.

Marble, marble everywhere, but because it is light in character and color and combined with white lacquer and glass-fronted cabinetry, the eye is drawn to the book-matched panel above the far sink, the room's built-in artwork. The light above the island adds an appealingly unexpected note.

PREVIOUS PAGES, ABOVE, AND OPPOSITE: You know you're in California when your kitchen has an abundance of light and space, indoor-outdoor flow, and a shaped ceiling—plus midcentury chairs. What makes this room distinctive is the detailing, which is highly particular (note the wall and ceiling lighting components) and, in the case of the glass box enclosing the range vent, unexpected.

This kitchen's muscular rusticity derives from its materiality: a beamed ceiling showing the effects of time, the textured irregular stone walls, a floor that's ready for anything. The utilitarian table and tacked chairs contribute to the idea, as does the nothing-to-hide refrigerator, but the niches above the cabinetry inject a more distinctly decorative note.

# The Importance of Touch

Of course, there is the moment when all of the remembering and fantasizing must coalesce into an architectural reality. Now the question arises: how to begin a practical nuts-and-bolts design process without losing contact with your kitchen's personal character? To this I can offer a one-word response: *touch*.

There are people whose idea of the perfect kitchen is literal perfection—a pristine environment in which you can not only dice carrots, but also conceivably perform surgery. At the other end of the scale, we find those for whom a kitchen isn't alive unless it's a cacophony of foods, aromas, and utensils—a splendid mess. But one maxim applies to both styles and to every preference in between: though all of the senses come into play, one's primary experience of the kitchen is tactile. Thus the elements on which you lay your hands, the surfaces and finishes and hardware, must deliver physical as well as functional reassurance, and of a sort specifically suited to you.

This principle is called *aesthetics of use*, and we already instinctively employ it when assembling a wardrobe. In the closet, we keep elegant outfits that come out once or twice a year for special occasions. And then there are the clothes we actually *live* in: a uniform of our own devising that's comfortable, useful, durable, personal, and effortlessly stylish. Once we hit on a wardrobe that works in all these ways, in which we are at home, we never take it off. And why should we? It feels good, looks good, and, best of all, it *works*.

You don't slip on a kitchen the way you do a sweater, but the same sensibility applies to the things on which you put your hands. The work surfaces, for example: whether you choose marble or butcher block, you want your countertops to be pleasing to the eye, feel satisfying to the touch, stand up to what you expect of them, and—critically, crucially—get better, in all respects, with age. Whether it's stone or metal or lacquer or paint, you want the material to patinate and acquire character rather than wear out or look cheap; if the surface is wood, you want to cherish the finger marks and knife scars, the physical record of satisfying use. Everyone admires objects of beauty and enjoys displaying them. But that's different from what might be described as the *companionship* one develops with a much-loved tool, which is what we seek in a kitchen. The room should feel as reliable, well made, and perfectly fitted as a tempered-steel carving knife or an English saddle.

In one respect, the kitchen is like every other room in one's home:
very little is required to make a moment of beauty and
serene repose other than a few precious things artfully arranged.

Here is a small urban-apartment kitchen in which little attempt has been made, beyond the introduction of the marble, to create decorative gestures. Yet this serves to make the kitchen more of a piece with the adjoining living space, and vice versa—you don't feel as if you live in the kitchen or are preparing food in the sitting room.

A good way to begin is to visit a kitchen showroom, which, in my experience, is always a great source of ideas and inspiration. Most feature vignettes that combine multiple components in different ways, allowing you to see and experience a range of possibilities in three dimensions. Well-equipped kitchen showrooms also have samples of their surfaces (stone, tile, and paint), cabinetry, and hardware on hand, so if a particular layout strikes your fancy but you want to try it with different elements, you can. You can also gather your selections in a three-dimensional mood board to make sure that they mix in an appealing way.

Visiting a kitchen showroom can also help you launch an inquiry into style (assuming you haven't thought about it already). As the images in this book proclaim, there are a nearly uncountable number of design directions in which to go. While you may begin with broad strokes—midcentury modern, let's say, or French country—the great laying on of hands that takes place in a kitchen showroom will encourage you to particularize, to make the room your own. A style choice is only a beginning. The fun comes when, as with a recipe, you doctor it and add the flourishes that mark it indelibly as *your creation*.

By designing your kitchen in this intuitive way, you'll create a space that gets better with age, is highly particular to your family, and encourages memory making—a room that seamlessly unites style and experience while also freeing you from being sidetracked by decisions, like modern versus traditional, that will ultimately make themselves. And now, having considered matters of style, let's move on to substance: it's time to drill down from macro to micro and discover how to make your kitchen not only beautiful, but also optimally functional.

This kitchen's design evinces a North African influence, evident in the lanterns, backsplash tiles, and perforated cabinet fronts, reminiscent of moucharaby windows, but it's also an illustration of the value of repetition, in both pattern and color.

What is interesting about this kitchen, which is insistently—indeed defiantly—monochrome and "correct," is that it stands as the quiet prelude to an explosion of radiant color and eccentric design.

OPPOSITE AND ABOVE: This kitchen uses two closely related but not identical shades of blue to produce two effects: introduce a note of traditional elegance and deliver a surprise.

Color in this context is used
not only to enliven a monochrome room, but also
to create an unexpected,
slightly surreal surprise.

The idea of casual dining has been turned on its head in this kitchen via the introduction of half a dozen luxurious leather-upholstered stools arranged around one end of a marble-topped island.

Kitchen floors don't always get a lot of attention—the action tends to be above ground level. The design of this space makes the point that an interesting floor plane can serve as an anchor for all of a kitchen's elements *and* provide the standout decorative element.

OPPOSITE: In this simple, unpretentious country kitchen, the utilitarian yet graceful gooseneck faucets, finished in nickel, set the tone. Glass-fronted cabinets, white tile, and a lightly figured marble contribute to the calm and welcoming environment—a lovely setting in which to prepare meals large and small, or to simply hang out. ABOVE: The combination pantry and bar continues the kitchen's color and material palettes.

Banquette seating is not traditionally associated with freestanding-island dining. The introduction of a tall, high-backed settee (supported by lemon-yellow stools) serves as a faux banquette and adds a note of restrained elegance.

There is much to admire in this comfortable combination of kitchen and family room—in particular the layering of a shaped, honed marble backsplash on a gleaming tile wall.

Another California kitchen, with an island suitable for landing a small aircraft. Apart from embracing the pleasures of the outdoors, the design, in its vertical and horizontal elements, captures the distinctive planar character of postwar West Coast modernism.

Developer architecture is rarely inspirational. Yet here, the design borrows from the building's structural character, at once utilitarian and volumetric, to reinterpret key traditional kitchen elements—the island and its illumination—in sculptural forms that might have suited Stanley Kubrick at his most futuristic.

ABOVE AND OPPOSITE: Though one may be hesitant to make an irrevocably bold choice in the kitchen, the virtues of so doing can be seen here. The copper sinks, range hood, back-splashes, pendant lights, and cabinet handles raise the impact of potent materiality to a new level. What's more, as these surfaces patinate, they will not only become more textured, tactile, and vivid, they'll also serve as a living, ever-changing record of the room's use.

The particular appeal of this kitchen, to my eye, is that it is grown-up and elegant and simultaneously young and hip. The marble supplies the chic, but the simplicity of the faucet, the absence of cabinet hardware, and, especially, the choice of color give the room an unmistakably downtown vibe.

82

ABOVE AND OPPOSITE: This is a small space in which, wondrously, the design team has inserted a plethora of program: in addition to the ultra-compact kitchen, the room contains a dining area, a living room, a wet bar, and a library with working fireplace—not to mention adjacency to the outdoors. I *love* the light fixture above the island.

ABOVE: Absent that space-age red light, the slab cabinet doors and restaurant-kitchen stainless-steel counters might seem to lack life. Instead, the room is young and fun.
OPPOSITE: When I was a child, two elements that could be found in the most "everyday" household kitchens were red Formica cabinetry and cork floors. Here, these building blocks of yesteryear have been updated most stylishly; as an especially clever addition, one side of the island morphs into the back of the banquette.

The charm of this room derives from the sense that, prior to becoming a kitchen, it might have been put to another use. Rather than being a liability, the relaxed, somewhat deconstructed character of the space—the open shelves, hanging copper pots, cutting boards tucked in a corner—make it ideal for a family hangout.

OPPOSITE AND ABOVE: Though this brings to mind what used to be called "parkitecture"—the style found in the national-park lodges built in the early twentieth century—it is, in fact, a private home in New York's Catskill mountain region. Every choice is robust, from the dramatically active stone to the brass-bound cooking machines to the woven leather on the chairs. The rooms—the kitchen and butler's pantry (complete with rotisserie) behind it—exude exuberance and, appropriately, appetite.

ABOVE AND OPPOSITE: I truly adore this kitchen, constructed almost entirely from thin sheets of plate steel and polished concrete, which feels like a Richard Serra sculpture within the larger volume of the house. Though everything about the room is physically hard, the design's originality and daring make it feel cool and, indeed, swank.

This lovely kitchen demonstrates that a sophisticated design can be constructed from elements that might be characterized as homespun. Why not decorate your wall with an arrangement of simple tools and warm up the space with rugs?

ABOVE AND OPPOSITE: Muscular marble extravagantly deployed, fixtures that demand to be noticed, an industrial-strength oven, and, in the midst of it, an exquisite Biedermeier-style table to remind us that, in every environment, there is always space for delicacy and taste.

ABOVE: I love the idea of using patterned tile in an unexpected place—the effect is lively and chic. Here, it reminds me of the lavish displays you see on the sides of buildings in Latin America and the Caribbean (and, for that matter, Miami). OPPOSITE: The lightly beamed ceiling helps to both zone the room and give scale to an unusually long island.

The "springing legs" supporting this island, reminiscent of the work of the contemporary French artist Xavier Veilhan, add a piquant note of the surreal to this traditional kitchen and distract from the size and bulk of the volume.

OPPOSITE AND ABOVE: There is nothing so utilitarian or insignificant that it
can't contribute to a moment of beauty—be it a rolling pin, a cutting board,
an old-fashioned scale, or a casually arranged display of colorful tomatoes.

The continuous floor and complementary color palette connect this kitchen to its adjoining spaces. The dark floor forms a strong ground for the white-painted cabinetry, and the lamps flanking the stove and slipcovered chairs add a note of tradition, rendered informally.

ABOVE AND OPPOSITE: This simple country kitchen is made elegant by the handling of its materials, the simplicity of the lighting and hardware choices, and the urbane yet warm quality of its decorative restraint.

# Julia Turshen

## COOKBOOK AUTHOR

I never had an Easy-Bake Oven. As a kid obsessed with cooking, I went straight for the real thing. With the supervision and support of my parents and babysitter, I was able to be in the kitchen (a real-life kitchen!) from an early age. As an adult who writes cookbooks for a living and cooks at home daily, I've spent a lot of time thinking about what has always drawn me to the kitchen with a pull I can only describe as magnetic. It hasn't just been the place where I feel excited (cooking is fun!) and where I learn so much: it's ultimately where I feel most *safe*.

Chopping vegetables, rotating sheet pans of cookies, gently simmering chicken bones in water, and kneading dough are all things that make me feel grounded, connected, and secure. The kitchen is where I start tasks and finish them. Where I cook for the people I love. Where I have the freedom to make a mess and the ability to clean up after it. Where I have a sense of control in a world that can feel overwhelming and scary, often at the same time.

I have cooked in many kitchens. The first was the galley kitchen in a Manhattan apartment where I was born, the next a larger suburban kitchen that went through a renovation, so I spent some time cooking in a makeshift kitchen set up in a bathroom with a microwave, toaster oven, and hot plate. I made meals in my summer-camp bunk and in the tiny kitchen in the common area of my college dormitory (yes, I brought a toolbox of kitchen utensils along with my books and extra-long twin bedsheets). I've cooked outdoors with no kitchen, including one time on a beach in South Korea. When I worked as a private chef, I cooked in some of the fanciest home kitchens you could imagine. Every Thursday morning, my wife, Grace, and I roll up our sleeves in a church kitchen—a church we don't belong to—as regular volunteers for an organization that provides homemade meals for homebound clients.

All of these experiences make me incredibly grateful that my favorite kitchen I've ever cooked in, hands down, is the one I get to cook in every single day. It's the kitchen in the house my wife and I live in with our many pets. It's not a new kitchen. It has been lived in and feels that way. I like that. Many of our pots, pans, and dishes have been handed down, making each meal an opportunity to remember the people who gave them to us. There's often music playing and lots of light coming in through the windows. It's got a door to the backyard that we open frequently to let our dogs in and out of and one toward the front that we use as our front door even though we have an actual front door.

But we skip the real front door because the way into our home is through our kitchen.

# Melissa Clark

## *NEW YORK TIMES* FOOD REPORTER

I live in Prospect Heights, Brooklyn, in a very narrow 1893 brownstone—it's only 14.9 feet wide. The kitchen is about 12 feet by 15 feet, but it's on the parlor floor in back, so it gets great natural light, overlooks the garden, and has access to the deck, where I keep my herbs.

We redid the kitchen about ten years ago, when I was pregnant with my daughter, which is a great time to do heavy renovations! My favorite element is the central island, which has a marble top. Everyone said don't do marble, it stains and it pits. But I thought about all those churches in Italy with marble steps, and all those café tables in Paris, and you know what? I think they look fantastic—they've got personality. Ten years in, the marble is a bit stained and chipped, and it's just beautiful. The island is pretty big—there's enough room for two stools on the end, and my husband often sits there when I cook and reads to me; we're reading the Emily Wilson *Odyssey* right now.

The other great thing about my kitchen is that even though it's small, I can still entertain. I like to have people with me when I cook, everyone around the island, and spilling out into the stair hall.

I have to admit, we made a mistake on the floor by choosing eco-friendly boards made out of cocoa-palm wood. They're stained really dark, and at the beginning they looked fine. But the staining came off quickly, and every time you drop something, it dents. We should have gone for reclaimed wood, but we'd have to rip out the floor to replace it, so that's not an option.

To me, the most important thing in a kitchen is flow. You have to know how you cook and how you want to use the space. I knew that I didn't want the sink in the center island, because if it's filled with dirty dishes, your guests can't gather round. This is going to sound silly, but you should also put in a broom closet—you'll need it. You need places to hide things you don't want people to see. I believe very strongly in a mix of open and closed cabinets.

Sometimes you'll see a little drawer that pulls out next to the stove, with niches for wine or spices. That's the worst possible place for those things, because the heat of the stove is going to ruin them. When you're designing, all your food needs to be on the cool side of the kitchen, and your pots and pans and dishes can be on the warmer side. It's these seemingly little things that make a big difference.

Knowing where you're going to put stuff before you start building takes time and effort, but it's worth it—you're going to use your kitchen forever. I would say that anyone who loves to cook and doesn't know quite how they want to use the space should talk to a kitchen designer. They think of things that architects might not.

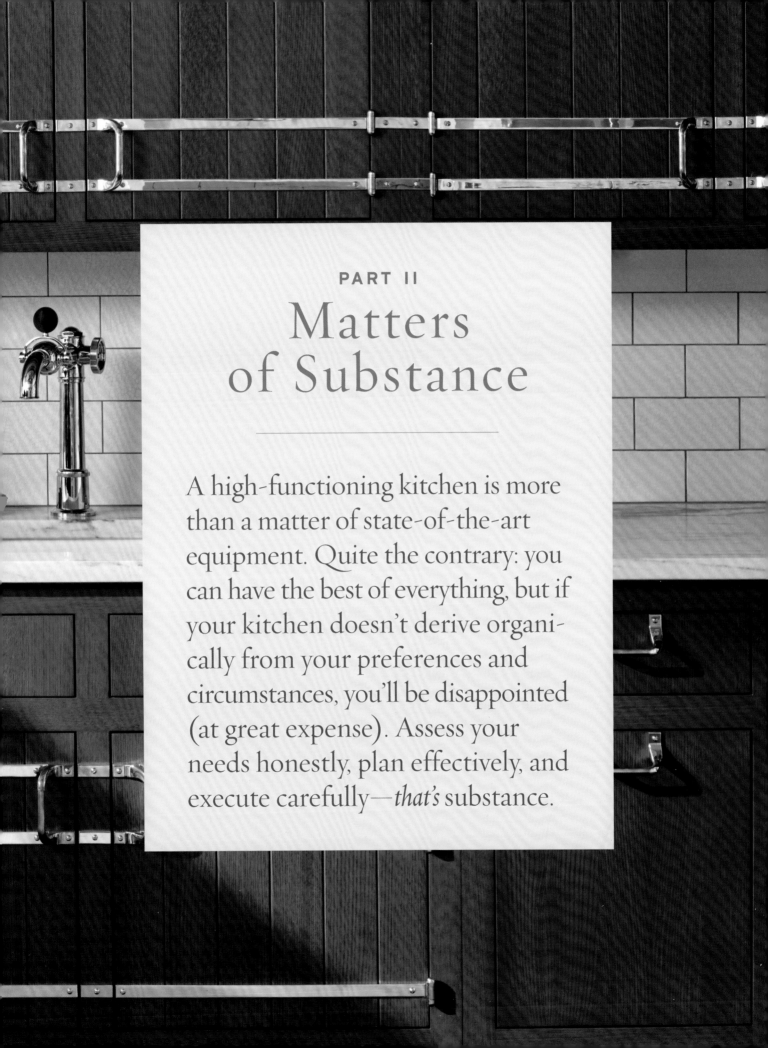

## PART II

# Matters of Substance

A high-functioning kitchen is more than a matter of state-of-the-art equipment. Quite the contrary: you can have the best of everything, but if your kitchen doesn't derive organically from your preferences and circumstances, you'll be disappointed (at great expense). Assess your needs honestly, plan effectively, and execute carefully—*that's* substance.

# Prioritize Personal
# Preference

The word *functionality* lacks the intimate character we ascribe to issues of style. Yet when thinking about how you want your kitchen to function, the first question to ask yourself is a highly personal one: what are my preferences?

Do you like to cook, and, if so, what sort of cook are you? A dabbler who views food primarily as sustenance? A gifted amateur who enjoys trying out new recipes twice a week? A parent feeding voracious teenagers? A professional with an expansive palate and skills to match?

Next, consider your circumstances. Is it just you cooking, or do you have helpers? How big is your family? Do you like to entertain? Do you have someone who comes in to prepare meals for you? Your circumstances also mean your physical situation, whether it's a country kitchen, a galley kitchen, a stand-alone kitchen, a kitchen with adjacent support spaces (pantry, mudroom, laundry, butler's pantry, bar), or a kitchen that opens onto a dining area or family room. Weigh the strengths and shortcomings of your setup. Can you build your kitchen from scratch and arrange it entirely to your liking, or is it in a city apartment with immovable water and gas lines? Are there windows? Views? Natural ventilation? The permutations are many, and each comes with its own set of requirements, all of which must be thoroughly, honestly addressed.

At this point, given the challenges of effective planning, you may be contemplating a life of takeout. But once you begin the journey, you'll find that you can get your arms around the task fairly quickly. One useful suggestion for sorting it all out: *get help.*

PREVIOUS PAGES: The inspiration for the bold brass strapping and integrated stirrup-like handles came from the fittings found in equestrian iconography. OPPOSITE: The scale of this kitchen is daunting, but the low fixture above the islands restores a measure of intimacy to the principal work zone.

# Don't Try This Alone

While there is a great deal one can do on one's own when it comes to planning and furnishing your space, I'm a big believer in working with a kitchen consultant to achieve the best possible outcome. As I observed in the introduction, the kitchen remains the most complicated room in the house in terms of its requirements, multiple uses, and aesthetics. Having an experienced professional on your side not only saves you time and helps you avoid costly mistakes, it also has a significant side benefit, too: right from the start, it lowers your anxiety about the project, since you can feel confident that you're making the right decisions.

I've spoken with many people who say, in effect, "I'm clueless, I have no idea of what I want, and I can't imagine where to begin." In fact, you know more—much more—than you realize. Tell me about the kitchen you have now—what are the pain points? Do the refrigerator and dishwasher doors collide when they're both open? Are you losing precious counter space to appliances because you have no place to stow them? Are the cabinets too high for you to comfortably access your everyday table settings? Conversely, what pleases you about your current setup? Can you look out a window when you're at the sink? Do you enjoy having a separate oven and cooktop? Simply enumerating the good and bad aspects of your present circumstances can reveal how much or little you want or need to innovate.

Another virtue of engaging a consultant is found in the maxim "You don't know what you don't know." A professional will invariably raise issues and draw on resources that we'd never consider on our own. This is particularly the case with regards to storage needs and patterns of use in your kitchen. It can be as simple as having someone inventory your dishes, flatware, and pots and pans, so you know precisely how much square footage you need—especially useful if your kitchen is tight and has limited growth potential. If your space is roomy, your consultant can guide you with pointed questions. For instance, do you want two sinks—one for cooking, another for cleanup—and if so, how big and in what proximity? I've had people tell me that while they initially found all of this cross-examination to be irritating and intrusive, they ultimately discovered needs and considerations that were unique to their circumstances—and had never entered their minds. The ability to not only ask the right questions, but also listen closely and interpret the answers, is a kitchen consultant's greatest asset.

This seemingly decorative tableau reveals one of the ways in which every part of a kitchen can be put to good use. The open shelves are both pleasing to behold and well stocked; under-counter lighting gives a theatrical character to essential goods. The photograph adds to the aesthetic effect, but the reality is all business.

I admire how this kitchen has been artfully woven into and around the building's structural elements—the outcome feels inevitable rather than forced.

Close questioning also helps produce a kitchen that fits the lifestyles of its occupants. A woman who enjoys spending time in the kitchen with her grandchildren, for example, has a host of considerations. Can the food-preparation zone be connected to an informal dining area? Is there room for the kids to help out safely and enjoyably?

Oftentimes, new spaces find their way into the planning process. In the course of discussions, you might mention a nearby closet that can be transformed into storage, or an adjacent mudroom that might double as a cleanup area or a place for flower arranging. (Yes, that's part of a kitchen's program, too.) The more you explore, the greater the range of possibilities—and the fewer the design mistakes.

Let me add that kitchen consultants tend to be very good at coordinating the various trades, from the electrician to the contractor to the tile installer—a big plus when it comes to staying on schedule and on budget. I will have more to say about this in the next chapter, but it can't be repeated too often: Whatever you create, no matter how perfect the design or how right the style, you'll never love it if the process of making it goes poorly and the finished product doesn't meet your expectations. If, on the other hand, you get the best people, their work is staged properly, and the time is taken to get it all right, you'll love your kitchen that much more. And the ultimate responsibility for this is yours—ask for references before beginning and check and re-check the work as it progresses. You'll never regret it.

A consultant can also help you with one of the trickiest aspects of kitchen design: stress-testing your wish list against spatial limitations and obstacles. In a typical urban apartment, the systems can't be moved, and the building has rules about what you can and cannot do. ("We're not allowed to swap our dishwasher for a miniature washer/dryer" is one I hear frequently.) In larger spaces unrestricted by co-op boards, other kinds of challenges emerge: for instance, how do you arrange the building blocks required to prepare meals in a way that suits your preferences *and* takes maximum advantage of light, air, and views? Even in the tiniest galley kitchen, good consultants can carve out surprisingly abundant space for storage, food prep, and appliances. Conversely, in big kitchens, they ensure a layout that flows naturally and inevitably while capitalizing on the room's expansiveness. Think of them as cooks who stir the alphabet soup of your circumstances until arriving at the message you want to receive.

In short, an experienced, talented specialist who listens carefully to your input will help you create a room that is maximally functional, good-looking, long-lasting, and, consequently, deeply satisfying to inhabit. Let the right one into your life, and you'll never regret it.

OPPOSITE: This space is an object lesson in how a carefully planned and programmed kitchen can incorporate a multitude of functions and elements with elegance and a seeming lack of effort. FOLLOWING PAGES: This is an exceptionally well-equipped and well-arranged kitchen, in which multiple cooks can work simultaneously. Two elements of note, one functional, the other aesthetic: the pot racks flanking the stove remind us that these useful components needn't hang from the ceiling. And the unusual beaming of the ceiling contributes a strong architectural note.

# Hands-On

Though I grew up in an analog world, I am as enamored of the digital life as the next person. Still, I'm leery of the idea of purchasing a kitchen online. Under certain circumstances, it may be the only option, of course, but this takes us back to a point I made in the previous chapter: in the kitchen, touch matters more than in any other room in the house—more, even, than in that most intimate of realms, the bath. Think about it: how many times a day do you turn your kitchen faucets on and off, open and close the cabinets and drawers, and mess up and wipe down the countertops? Your connection with each of those experiences is, first and foremost, tactile, and if you don't like the feel of a lever, pull, finish, or material, your kitchen will never be truly *yours*—some subtle, unmistakable disconnect will always be embedded in it. For this reason, once you and your kitchen consultant have come up with a plan, it's essential that you visit a showroom and touch everything. You can see what you're getting, more or less, on a computer screen. But it's impossible to understand the properties of a material, the temperature of a color, the reflectivity of a finish, or the ergonomic friendliness of a drawer pull unless you experience them in person.

As with virtual dating, the kitchen pictures you see online don't tell a complete story. There's no substitute for a real-life encounter.

The slab doors and vertical and horizontal planes here derive warmth and character via the careful handling of the wood—an example of how a plain working kitchen can be made special by selecting the right material. Fitting the breakfast table into the crook of the L-shaped island adds interest and saves space.

OPPOSITE AND ABOVE: A simple wood-and-white painted kitchen, made serenely beautiful by the scale of the architecture. The shaped marble behind the stove resolves an ordinarily featureless design moment with elegance. The dining niche is both light-filled and cozy.

The light-colored millwork and handsomely figured marble combine with a contemporary artwork and stylish black pottery—and the connection to the family room—to make this simple kitchen feel comfortable, youthful, and chic.

# Other Design Professionals

Whether you're renovating an existing kitchen, building a kitchen from scratch, or tearing out what you've got and installing something new, your interactions will probably be limited to a kitchen consultant and a contractor. Yet your kitchen resides within the larger context of a home. Consequently, it might be one component of a more comprehensive architecture or design project. Depending on their level of experience, practitioners in those fields may be able to create a kitchen that's perfectly tailored to your wants and needs. If not, you may choose to bring a kitchen consultant on board to work with your architect, decorator, or, upon occasion, both.

When it comes to the kitchen, in my experience, architects and designers have different strengths. Architects are good at helping you get the most out of your space, at making sure that the kitchen relates comfortably to adjacent rooms, and at ensuring that it occupies the right position within the overall scheme of your home. Decorators are better able to link the particulars of your kitchen to your home's overall aesthetic narrative. A kitchen consultant can interact with either or both design professionals in ways large and small. If an architect or decorator has already worked closely and successfully with a client on a kitchen's layout and components, a kitchen consultant may simply advise on fittings, finishes, and cabinetry selections. At the other end of the scale, he or she may contribute extensive expertise to the project to ensure that the end result is equally functional and beautiful.

This simply designed kitchen contains a single decorative element: the freestanding table adjacent to the island (and precisely the same height). The drawers and lower shelf give the piece its functionality.

This kitchen, a bit on the formal side and resembling a living room, is in fact versatile and well equipped, with a pot filler above the stove and multiple choices for dining—a good mix of beauty and utility.

# Fail to Plan, Plan to Fail

As that last point suggests, when it comes to the creation of a successful kitchen, planning is absolutely indispensable. There are two sides to it. One might be described as technical: accurate measurements, proper specifications, a realistic timetable, making sure the plumber shows up before the carpenter. The other—no less critical—side is *listening*. Each of us has dealt with a professional, whether a garage mechanic or a dental surgeon, who only half paid attention to our complaints, diagnosing the problem before giving a full and thoughtful hearing to the symptoms. And we all know how *that* turned out (at great expense, the engine still knocked, the tooth still throbbed).

There is very little margin for error in the creation of a successful kitchen. So it remains *essential* that when you describe what it is that you want, your architect, decorator, or kitchen consultant listens thoroughly and analytically to what you have to say, and that any areas of uncertainty are fully, honestly resolved before the first screw is turned. Otherwise, you will be disappointed—again, at great expense.

And remember, the person who has to listen most closely is you, to others and to yourself. Though you may not think so, ultimately, you know best.

# Time

Apart from budget ("*That's* how much this will cost?!"), perhaps the biggest misperception people have about kitchens is how long they take to create. Even experienced architects and designers can be brought up short—assuming that a job can progress from preliminary sketches to the punch list in three months, only to discover, after talking the project through with a kitchen consultant, that what they're really looking at is closer to six months or even a year. Scheduling can be particularly hard on civilians who, upon seeing an agreeable vignette in a showroom, assume that something comparable can be installed in their home between Labor Day and Thanksgiving. If what matters most is the meeting of a hard target date, almost anything is possible—but only if you're prepared to make compromises. A case in point: hand-painted cabinets look wonderful but require execution, curing, and drying processes that simply can't be rushed; if your timetable doesn't allow for that, you may have no choice but to accept factory-finished ones. And that is but one of a multitude of time-centered considerations.

Sticker shock is almost always a bit of an issue, but don't be surprised if the time required delivers an even bigger jolt.

Three gestures make this kitchen feel bold and original: the patterned wood of the island; the graphic character of the tile; and the matte-finished charcoal-colored cabinetry.

132

How do you transform the simplest of kitchens into a showplace? By insisting upon absolute precision and introducing a single arresting element—in this case, the pristine fixture above the island.

# Design Development

The most effective antidote to the pains of both budget and schedule? An efficient design process. Every kitchen designer or consultant has a particular approach, but for all of us making or redoing a kitchen, the steps remain largely the same: once the team has completed the extensive talking-and-listening phase and collected all of the necessary technical, spatial, and logistical information, the next step is the initial presentation drawings. Surprisingly, if you've been conscientious about all of the preliminaries, that first pass should be very close to the finished product. In our experience, it's unusual for someone to tear everything up and start again from scratch; more typically, clients will want to revisit ideas that are being presented for the first time or make cosmetic adjustments. After that initial review, two or three rounds of changes are usually sufficient to arrive at a final iteration, after which your designer can proceed to detailed technical drawings, confirm costs, and prepare to go into production. While minor tweaks can be made after preproduction has begun—for instance, adding a drawer to a cabinet—anything major, once the trigger has been pulled, is strongly discouraged. When the kitchen design has been finalized, so has your approximate delivery date, and the schedule will be pulled apart by any sort of significant changes.

I am, of course, making this sound problem-free, and no construction project in the history of the human race has ever been so. But good communication, meticulous planning, triple-checking, and conscientious follow-through produce a satisfying, successful outcome more often than not.

In this relatively small kitchen with a minimum of storage space, the impact derives from two lighting elements. One is the rectangle above the island, which bathes the room in sunshine. The other is the trio of pendants hung from the world's biggest angle irons.

# No Island Is an Island

Sometimes it can take a while to see what's plain as day. For example, I was nearly finished compiling the images for this book before I noticed that almost every kitchen contained an island. I suppose it has to do with the fact that these volumes have become so commonplace that they seem no more exceptional than ovens. And yet my abrupt awareness of their ubiquity reminded me that, not so very long ago, islands were oddities. Where did they come from, and how have they managed to assume such an indispensable position in our kitchens' lives?

I trace the advent of the island to two factors: the rise of the kitchen as a flexible social space and an ever-increasing emphasis on high functionality. The island remains a natural gathering place nonpareil, democratizing the kitchen in both directions: the preparation of a meal, on full display, ceases to be a Wizard of Oz-like mystery; and the cook (or cooks) can engage with friends and family and participate in the experience of an occasion. At the same time as its magnetic properties draw us together socially, the island stands as an expression of a kitchen's capacities: it can serve as little more than a tall table or be action-packed, incorporating sinks, storage, cooktops, dishwashers, and even feeding stations for pets. As more of us opt for open kitchens that communicate with other spaces, islands have also come to serve an architectural function, creating a demarcation between working and living zones. Though we perhaps register this fact unconsciously, islands enable us to understand how rooms should be used.

Things often disappear or appear organically in response to circumstances. Once *Homo sapiens* left the water and the trees, we lost our tails. Conversely, as the void space in a kitchen's middle became populous and consumer technology offered up machines in need of a place to nest, presto! The island appeared—never, I suspect, to go away.

If I told you that I planned to tile my kitchen entirely in black, it might give you pause, but when combined with whitewashed wood, exposed shelves, and an abundance of natural light, the outcome owns the no-nonsense appeal of a working farm.

This high-end "system" kitchen is as impersonal as one you'd find in a catering hall. Yet the trio of Cherner chairs, with their ginkgo leaf-shaped backs; the red-lacquered tea set; and the adjacent sitting area with shelves displaying black pots transform the experience into something unexpectedly gracious and serene.

# Cost Control

There is no getting around the fact that kitchens are expensive. Nonetheless, as with all construction projects, there is a path to intelligent value engineering, one influenced in this case by the highly personal relationship between a kitchen and the person or persons who will be using it.

Because a successful kitchen is one that's maximally functional, it's best to err on the side of excess while you're still in the early design stages. Include the drawers with flexible dividers, the racks for hanging stemware, the bespoke knife storage (rather than just presenting a lot of undifferentiated shelf and storage space), and then decide what's really essential. I've seen people go in both directions: sometimes it's "That's more than I wanted to spend, but I know it'll be worth it"; other times I hear, "I can live without this and save myself $10,000." But I've also observed that once a project is finished, no one *ever* goes back to improve the quality of something on which they never should have economized in the first place. Which leads to one of my ironclad rules: invest in the highest quality you can afford, especially when it comes to the things you can't change, like cabinets. Sticking with the best is something one very seldom regrets.

A lot of back-and-forth is required before deciding on the right cost-to-need ratio. But in the end, it guarantees a kitchen that is exceptionally well considered, and that does precisely what you wish it to do.

This kitchen might make you feel as if you've been wrapped in a grape leaf. But to me, the bold color statement in a small galley space gives the room a jolt of urbane glamour.

The striped slipcovers
and wall-mounted
baskets conspire
with the light and
views to make this
relaxed country
kitchen feel at once
welcoming and utterly
without pretense.

# Mistakes We Make,
## Items You Love

Despite this know-it-all image I have sketched, kitchen designers and consultants are not, in fact, infallible. Indeed, there is one rather surprising error to which we are consistently susceptible: becoming so involved in getting the kitchen right that we overlook the limitations of its surroundings. Take high-rise apartment buildings: it's easy to forget that ceilings can be lower than expected, hallways and doorways narrow, elevators too confined, stairways too twisty. You create the perfect kitchen, and then you can't get it past the threshold! Many a kitchen designer has learned the hard way (and more than once) the importance of making a close study of the unalterable circumstances that can impact an installation.

We've also been surprised by some of the items that please clients the most. A much-beloved innovation is the under-the-counter dish drawer, with movable pegs that can be arranged to accommodate all of your place settings. It's a great way to organize and protect your plates. And as architects and decorators have increasingly begun to design kitchens without wall-mounted cabinets—the better to leave room for windows—the dish drawer has transformed from a novelty into a necessity. Finally, it seems like a small item, but everyone loves it: the drawer above the garbage can that holds the trash bags.

It is a lot to take in, I know. But if there's one piece of advice that applies to everyone creating a kitchen, no matter his or her means or circumstances, it is this: take however much time you need to get it right, because once your kitchen is finished, there's no going back.

One might feel isolated in this white box if not for the continuous floor connecting to the house's social spaces and a framed view of an arresting work of art.

A lesson in how to make a minimalist modern kitchen into a
gathering space: pops of color,
chic seating, and a sun-washed
desert garden to attract the eye.

OPPOSITE: When a functional feature can also serve as a decorative statement, so much the better. Such is the case in this kitchen, in which the outsize industrial ventilation system contrasts dramatically with the rustic, rough-hewn setting. ABOVE: An abundance of natural light and handsome surface materials (the wood in particular) can distract you from how exceptionally well planned and well equipped this kitchen is.

151

ABOVE: The phrase "everything but the kitchen sink" comes to mind for this delightfully decorated tiny zone, with its pink tile, checkerboard floor, chandelier, diamond-patterned glass cabinet doors, and twin bunny-rabbit dish towels. *And* there's a kitchen sink. OPPOSITE: This small but smartly flowing kitchen makes no attempt to conceal its functionality, as the range vent makes plain, yet it still enjoys a sleek aesthetic and is crowned by a classic Serge Mouille light.

This kitchen is at once grand in scale and unpretentious in character. It makes good use of its generous space, enjoys natural light and green views, and can accommodate multiple cooks simultaneously while welcoming the individual. Its cheerfulness derives from the fact that every surface—floor, walls, cabinets, and ceiling—is painted an identical shade of white.

When the dining table stands between a kitchen's two stations, the best solution is to put it to work. Move aside the chairs, and this beautifully hewn and constructed piece of furniture becomes a generous island.

Formerly the open space between two cottages that were combined into a single residence, this galley kitchen has an appeal that derives from its enveloping glazed sliver of light, landscape, and sky.

Holding back the floor and ceiling
volumes from the walls gives
this basic kitchen, with its expansive
counter space, a sense of weight-
lessness. The connection to the
hallway and the room beyond
joins the kitchen with the larger
experience of the house.

The bin-pull handles, brass shelf brackets, and hanging cutting boards lend this kitchen the old-fashioned appeal of a general store. The lightness of the worktable makes for a refreshing alternative to the ubiquitous fixed island.

ABOVE: The openwork shelves connect this kitchen to the
living room and its windows. OPPOSITE: Another kitchen that
evokes a bygone era: that of the drugstore lunch counter.

This kitchen has been designed for two different experiences, which are reflected in the different character of the islands: the one near the windows, with stool seating and within reach of the coffeepot and toaster, is for breakfast and lunch. The larger one in the foreground, with more work space and a built-in sink, works the night shift.

ABOVE AND OPPOSITE: These appropriately minimalist
spaces defer to the big event: the view.

RIGHT: This notably urbane kitchen—the dramatically figured stone recalls the surfaces in the lobby of the Empire State Building, visible in the distance—also embraces a great country pleasure: a big sink with a window above it.
FOLLOWING PAGES: A kitchen that might otherwise feel imposing is humanized by the harmonious use of a restrained color and material palette.

# Pascale Le Draoulec

### FOOD WRITER AND FARMERS' MARKET DIRECTOR

I don't know if I have the "perfect" kitchen, but my kitchen makes me happy.

It isn't very big *by choice*. I prefer the intimacy of a smaller kitchen. My one requirement when we remodeled was that our family of five be able to cook, bake, or prep in the kitchen all at once and that we all be able to sit comfortably together. Helping with French homework or discussing the high-school musical while stirring risotto is good stuff. Space in our kitchen was too tight for a table with chairs, so we built a cozy bench into the wall.

It's important for me to have a radio for music and news. I also need art. Oil paintings, be they abstract or old-world, provide warmth, texture, and color in contrast to the "cool" feel of steel and marble and tile. Ditto for plants and herbs, which is why I made sure my windowsills were wide enough to hold a four-inch pot for succulents in the winter and herbs in the summer. A bunch of tulips or a bowl of clementines always anchors the island.

I like decanting pedestrian products into pretty vessels. I keep my cooking salt in a vintage, cracked piece of Quimper pottery; potatoes live in an old French wicker bicycle basket affixed to the wall in the pantry. My olive oil goes into a long-necked glass bottle I "thrifted" long ago. Such details help bring pleasure to something as mundane as dressing a salad or doing the dishes.

So does looking out the window onto our garden. We decided to keep all the windows at the expense of upper cabinets. No regrets. Birds over cupboards, *any* day.

I prefer open shelving anyway, especially for objects that are used every day: coffee mugs and cereal bowls and water glasses. Even better if these shelves are within easy reach of the dishwasher, as in our kitchen, and if you choose cups and bowls that make you smile.

Bright overhead lighting is important (make sure it's dimmable!), but soft, warm lighting is also essential in a kitchen. When you come downstairs late at night for a cup of Egyptian mint tea, you want a soft glow to lead you to the kettle. Late-night talks over a bowl of ice cream don't happen under harsh lights.

Everything should feel good in your hand, from your drawer pulls to the wooden spoons to the fabric of your dish towels to the chalk you use to scribble a shopping list on your chalkboard—another kitchen *must*.

Before this kitchen I'd never had an open pantry, and now that I have one, I don't know how I managed without one. I love my Weck jars, which come in so many perfect sizes for everything from dried figs to cornmeal to couscous, though it took a while to get used to their fiddly lids. Having everything on display keeps you honest.

I keep all my spices, even the more exotic ones, above my stove instead of in the pantry. I like to think that my glass jars of fennel seed and fenugreek keep me from falling into a rut.

174

# Alfred Portale

Though I'm a professional chef, I am, and have always been, interested in aesthetics. Before I started cooking, I aspired to be an artist, and this was followed by a flirtation with jewelry design. Today my interest in materiality and the intricacies of construction gets channeled into my hobby as an amateur woodworker: at home in Connecticut, I build objects and furniture out of refined and often exotic woods. Of course, my passion for the mechanics of making is on display nightly at my restaurant, where the application of a sauce, the swirl of a drizzle, receives the utmost attention.

In fact, the relationship between cooking and design influenced my kitchens in three different homes. In a New York apartment long ago, the cabinets were handmade from bird's-eye maple, and I built my own table and designed the banquette for the integrated dining area. My next home, on Long Island, featured zebrawood kitchen cabinets and drawers with carefully matched grains. In Connecticut, I finally had the opportunity to design the kitchen's layout, and I created a vast island, topped with inch-and-a-quarter-thick Carrara marble, that serves as a work surface, informal dining zone, and chef's table.

As that last function suggests, my kitchen remains an experiential and social, as well as a functional, space. When I am doing my thing, everyone wants to see how I do it—no doubt because I'm a professional—so I generally have an audience. Sometimes it's guests who congregate around the island with cocktails, but it can be family as well. Whatever the case, food preparation is seldom a solitary pursuit, and I wouldn't have it any other way.

When asked for suggestions about how to set up a kitchen, I first and foremost stress a good flow, but there are other significant considerations. I'm the kind of home cook who cleans as he goes, and for the sake of aesthetics and efficiency as well as tidiness, there's a slot on my countertop that lets me sweep the leavings directly into the trash. The drawers in which I store pots and pans are lined with stainless steel, to both protect the wood and make them easier to clean. I am a great believer in having two dishwashers, especially if you like to entertain. And *very* important is a second oven—a smaller electric one built into the island if possible. It comes in handy for warming, baking, and any occasion—think of Thanksgiving—when your primary oven is taken up with a single overwhelming object.

As for things to avoid, I'd suggest not making your kitchen too large. It's tempting, I know. But a big, cold space militates against companionability; compression equals intimacy. And stay away from malodorous gas grills, unless you want to spend your life fanning the smoke detector.

Of course, no kitchen has it all. I, for one, would love to enjoy an elevated wood-burning oven or fireplace for roasting, baking, or grilling. To have it fired up, especially in the cooler months, would be heaven. Maybe next time.

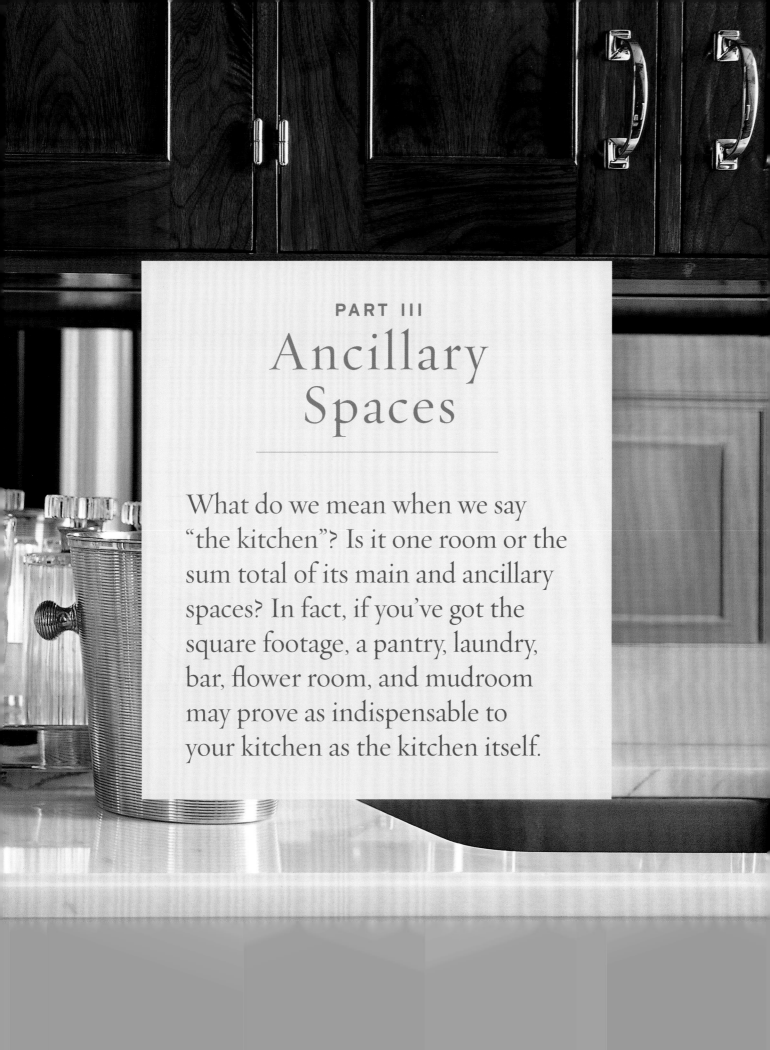

**PART III**

# Ancillary Spaces

What do we mean when we say "the kitchen"? Is it one room or the sum total of its main and ancillary spaces? In fact, if you've got the square footage, a pantry, laundry, bar, flower room, and mudroom may prove as indispensable to your kitchen as the kitchen itself.

# Other Needs, Other Rooms

This book is called *The Perfect Kitchen*, and, to be sure, that is our main focus. But just as the United States of America includes not only the fifty states, but also a number of territories that participate in the life of the nation, the kitchen is a domain comprising an essential room supported, to a greater or lesser degree, by any number of ancillary spaces.

The most significant of these is the pantry. Indeed, I heartily recommend devoting as much consideration to the planning of this zone—assuming you have the space for it—as to the kitchen itself. Often viewed as an afterthought or simply a place to stash canned goods and extra pet food, a well-considered pantry can serve as an able junior partner to a kitchen, combining the usual storage opportunities with food preparation, a staging area for serving, and shelves for cookbooks. Treat the pantry as a high-functioning, multi-various support space for the kitchen's main mission, and you will be surprised by how useful, even indispensable, it can be.

Other ancillary areas might include the laundry, the flower room, and that often undervalued but really indispensable component, the mudroom. The fact that each can be absorbed into the program of the kitchen suggests just how central the latter remains to the life of any home. Having intercommunicating kitchen and laundry spaces reminds us that domestic activities typically occur simultaneously. The availability of a flower room suggests that a kitchen is the room in which many forms of joy are created. And if you enter your kitchen through a mudroom, shedding boots, coats, and packages as you go, you know that more often than not, the first room you enter upon coming home is the kitchen.

Indeed, the kitchen *is* home, which is why making seamless connections to its satellite spaces is so significant.

This pantry evinces the appeal of a traditional general store, in which nearly everything remains on display and you can spot what you want at a glance. The industrial lighting and rolling ladder add to the room's all-business, no-nonsense character.

ABOVE: The postmodern backsplash panels flanking this interior window lend a traditional tableau a dash of the surreal. OPPOSITE: The lustrous black finish, mirrored backsplash, and glass-fronted cabinets give this bar a severe sophistication accented with a dash of glamour.

OPPOSITE: A freestanding hutch, with handsomely finished wood and bright marble, gives this spot a country character and sets it apart from its surroundings.
ABOVE: Artworks and objects, displayed on open shelves and moodily illuminated by a skylight, personalize a bar that's rich in color and materiality.

ABOVE: This simple, handsome bar area benefits from a generosity of counter and cabinet space. OPPOSITE: This butler's pantry restates the decorative motifs of the kitchen it accompanies (seen on pages 32-33) in simpler language appropriate to the relationship between the two rooms.

ABOVE AND OPPOSITE: As Americans' taste for fine wines and spirits
has evolved, so too has the design of the wine cellar and the bar.

OPPOSITE AND ABOVE: Dark wood, brass fixtures, glass-fronted cabinets, and marble can bestow a touch of class on the smallest and simplest of secondary spaces. I particularly enjoy the wood-and-brass hardware on the opposite page.

OPPOSITE: The choice of color gives this butler's pantry both formality and luxuriousness. The unexpected introduction of school lights seems entirely appropriate for a hallway work space. ABOVE: Color strikes again, turning this bar, tucked away in a niche, into a moment of funky radiance.

ABOVE: The brass bin-pull handles against handsomely sawn wood and the vertical blue boards wrap this transitional space in tradition. OPPOSITE: If you can work an architectural fragment into a design, the effect can be magical—and unique.

ABOVE: Slate, brick, and raw wood cast this space indelibly as a greenhouse.
OPPOSITE: The combination of found elements in this delightful rustic
space, deftly inserted into the architecture and augmented with quirky
decorative objets, makes for an especially inviting moment.

Open shelves and ample counter space permit the display of three collections in this generously scaled mudroom: earthenware pitchers, brass watering cans, and wicker baskets.

ABOVE: Two elements supply the surprise here: the rough-hewn wide plank floor and the grisaille artworks. OPPOSITE: Continuing the floor, materials, and counter height from the kitchen into the flower room creates continuity while establishing a basis for difference.

ABOVE: The surprising introduction of a formal antique table transforms the character of an otherwise utilitarian room. OPPOSITE: There is something sublimely satisfying about throwing in a load of laundry, and when you can do it in a chic, rustic setting like this, the task is extra pleasurable.

ABOVE AND OPPOSITE: One of the most dependable ways to bring even an undistinguished laundry room to life: a decoratively patterned floor.

# Brian McCarthy

## INTERIOR DESIGNER

The apartment I share with my partner, Danny, a typical New York "classic six," is in a 1922 building designed by Warren and Wetmore, the architects responsible for Grand Central Terminal. Our building is not quite *that* grand, but the lobby is a stately, elegant mix of neoclassical and art deco, which I fell in love with the first time I walked in.

Though I've redone the apartment several times, the kitchen remains almost precisely as I found it nineteen years ago—which is to say, perfectly organized. We've got the "golden triangle" between the stove, refrigerator, and sink; abundant counter space; and a tremendous amount of storage in both upper and lower cabinets. (There's also a combination pantry and bar as you enter the room.) If we're making a sit-down dinner for friends, there's ample space in which to prepare and plate; if a buffet's the thing, all of the serving dishes can be comfortably arranged on one side. My kitchen isn't beautiful—and someday I'll redo it—but no matter what happens cosmetically, I wouldn't change the layout in the least.

In fact, there's no reason why any kitchen, no matter the size or configuration, can't be efficient: you figure out what you need, assess the challenges and opportunities, and get the most out of what you've got. The key is to think about how the kitchen will be used. Will it be all about food preparation, or also a family room? Do you do your own cooking, or will others help? Once you've asked and answered the pertinent questions, the appropriate program will reveal itself.

My firm has designed a multitude of kitchens over the decades, yet we often engage storage planners to help us maximize space, and these canny consultants have taught me many tricks. One of the best: When people design cabinets, they typically opt for three shelves, but five is better—you won't have big, heavy stacks of china to move, and you can organize and access the contents more comfortably and efficiently. Think as well about setting your shelves on glides. That way, you can lay hands on all the tableware in back that you'd otherwise never use.

Maybe you don't cook much now, but that's never an excuse not to get the kitchen right. You might suddenly decide to start—and if not, the next owner will surely appreciate your efforts.

# Ellie Cullman

## INTERIOR DESIGNER

Food has always been an obsession in my family—the proof of which is that my dad purchased the famous Brooklyn steakhouse Peter Luger's in 1950. Not surprisingly, my idea of the perfect kitchen revolves around at-home hospitality: a surfeit of space in which my large family can gather for everyday meals and also help cook when we celebrate holidays and special events.

In my house in Stamford, Connecticut, we're always entertaining extended family on weekends, and we can have as many as forty guests on occasions such as Thanksgiving. The equipment, I'm happy to say, is up to the task: between the kitchen and the breakfast room, we are lucky enough to have three sinks in which to prepare fresh vegetables from the gardens, clean chickens from our coops, and arrange the abundant flowers that grow in our backyard. And the rectangular island, with access on all four sides, lets everyone help out. The lesson? Although one stovetop and two good ovens will always suffice, you can never have too many sinks.

As well as the requisite work triangle and super-sturdy granite countertops, my kitchen has personality yet doesn't clash with the rest of the home by introducing a different style. Closed, white-painted cabinets and holophane lights are complemented by weather vanes, stars, and World War I and II posters that reflect my love

of Americana, which is manifest in every other aspect of the house. I find closed cabinets especially useful to store china, vases, and serving pieces in my kitchen, where practicality and function never go out of style.

205

## PART IV
# Details

In matters great and small, there can be no macro without micro, and this is especially the case in the kitchen, in which the significance of the well-chosen detail cannot be overstated.

# A Million Little Things

Having looked at the kitchen and its handmaiden zones from the standpoints of both design and function, it is my hope that you've got your arms around the challenge—rather, the pleasure—of planning a space that, in all respects, is the ideal one for your situation. The only question that remains is, What are the component parts from which your perfect kitchen will be constructed?

You've heard all the clichés assigning ownership of details to God and/or the Devil, but between these otherworldly realms there is a simpler truth: the details are in *your* hands. And with sufficient information, they remain relatively easy to manage.

On the pages that follow, we have broken down the kitchen into its component parts and created comprehensive lists of options for each category, beginning with the most impactful and concluding with the small but significant choices that make a space such as this feel fully, satisfyingly complete. I will also show you the choices that my husband, Robert, and I made for our own kitchen, and how they coalesce.

Even the simplest kitchen represents a game of multiple choice, with considerations that include hardware, surfaces, and accessories.

# Cabinets & Hardware

Should we require evidence that today's kitchens are much more complex affairs than those of yesteryear, we need look no further than the cabinet. I've seen photos of a nineteenth-century Scandinavian farmstead in which there were none at all—at mealtimes, the farmer and his family simply took their single plate from a rack, sat down at the table, and ladled in the stew. Nor do we need to go back that far in time: I can remember family kitchens in which the cabinets were limited in number, devoid of any contents other than a few shelves, and entirely utilitarian in character.

No longer. Today the kitchen is an integral, highly visible part of the home, requiring case goods of the highest quality and look—when the kitchen came out of the aesthetic closet, aesthetic closets came into the kitchen. And given our multiple sets of dishes, flatware, glasses, and cooking and serving elements, their interiors are infinitely more elaborate.

Nor can cabinets be separated from their hardware. In addition to being a kitchen's jewelry, hardware must be multivalent: complementary to the case goods, comfortable to the hand, in keeping with the home and, indeed, its surroundings. All require consideration.

## CABINETS

**TYPE**
Traditional
    Complex moldings
    and trim
Transitional
    Simple panels
Modern
    Slab doors

**DOOR INSERTS**
Metal mesh
Chicken wire
Cane
Antique mirror

**FINISHES**
Paint
    Factory-applied
    Hand-painted
Stain
Metal

**OPTIONS**
Knife block
Spice insert
Pull-out pot storage
Peg-and-post dish dividers
Silverware tray
Diagonal utensil storage
Tray and cookie sheet dividers
Garbage receptacles with
    garbage-bag storage drawer
Produce bin
Appliance lift
Stainless dry-goods storage bin
Bread bin
Coffee station
Pet-feeding station

## HARDWARE

**TYPE**
Knobs
Pulls (cabinet and appliance)
Latches
Hinges
    Exposed
        Strap hinges
        Butterfly hinges
        H hinges
        Olive hinges
    Concealed
Shelf brackets

**FINISHES**
Brass
Nickel
Chrome
Matte nickel
Copper
Leather
Wood
Specialty

There may not always be room in a kitchen for a library, but with thoughtful planning, structural elements can become a repository for cookbooks.

OPPOSITE AND ABOVE: With their styles and finishes, cabinets establish the decorative tone of a kitchen and, not least, signal how the room is meant to be used, whether ambitiously and often, or as a place visited infrequently (and most often by a guest chef or caterer).

ABOVE AND OPPOSITE: Hardware can either reinforce or particularize the story told by the cabinetry or stand in counterpoint to it. And as with the jewelry that we choose to wear, a kitchen's hardware can offer the opportunity, within a simple setting, to make a statement, to innovate, or to be flashy.

ABOVE AND OPPOSITE: It isn't a stretch to say that the interior design of kitchen cabinetry can be as complex, craft-driven, and elegant as the interior design of an entire home. Everything matters, especially when you're crafting bespoke dividers for a multitude of drawers. You wouldn't think that the quality and personality of the wood you select for these hidden zones would make a difference, but believe me, when you pull open a cutlery drawer and find walnut instead of birch, you'll notice.

# Sinks & Faucets

If your kitchen's going to swim, it needs a great sink.

For me, the sink is the kitchen's hardest-working component. I must use mine fifty times a day, for everything from filling the teakettle to rinsing the lunch plates to washing the vegetables to pruning the flower stems. My husband uses it as a storage unit—until he's ready to load the dishwasher.

So ask yourself important questions. Do you want a sink big enough to wash a dog in or something more discreet? Metal, porcelain, or stone? A single basin, or one divided for food prep and dirty dishes? Are you zoned for a disposal? Can you accommodate two drains?

And—most important of all—what sort of faucet will you pair the sink with? If the sink is the body, the faucet is the animating brain. While looks matter, the functional choices you make will affect the experience of use indelibly. Consider the sink and faucet as a single element, one driven by your particular needs and patterns of use.

## SINKS

**MATERIALS**
Stainless steel
Fireclay
Cast iron
Marble
Unlacquered brass
Nickel
Copper

**TYPE**
Single-bowl
Double-bowl
Triple-bowl
Drainboard
Shelves

## FAUCETS

**TYPE**
Three-hole
Three-hole with spray
Single-hole
Single-hole with spray
Single-hole with pull-down spray
Two-hole with bridge
Two-hole bridge with spray
Pot filler (wall- or counter-mount)

Apart from the unmixed pleasure of throwing open one's windows onto a magnificent setting and washing the greens in a great big tub of a sink, I appreciate the gooseneck faucet that avoids obstructing the space beneath it and the special white quarter-round tiles that gracefully turn the corners on either side of the window.

222

ABOVE AND OPPOSITE: The five pictured here suggest the surprising variety
to be found within the world of the sink. Small differences in width and
depth can have a large impact on your experience of use. Your selection
of material can produce an effect ranging from quotidian to lush.

OPPOSITE AND ABOVE: Like sinks, faucets occur in a remarkable level of variety and, consequently, choice. The quantity and positioning of taps and valves and temperature controls, the height and flexibility and number of spouts—all open the mind to unexplored possibilities.

ABOVE AND OPPOSITE: Anyone who has ever staggered from sink to stove with a pot made heavy by gallons of liquid will appreciate the pleasures of the pot filler. These can be discreet and simple or as elaborate and flashy as something out of a Victorian firehouse. Whatever the case, a pot filler is a wonderfully worthwhile amenity.

# Islands

As noted previously, the island's ubiquity is a relatively recent phenomenon, yet its central importance to modern kitchen design is irrefutable. Islands, despite the apparent simplicity of the idea, are tricky because they can go in so many different directions. They can be casual, unprogrammed, and little more than a freestanding counter or table space. Or—more typically—islands can be heavily, even intensely, layered, with sinks, dishwashers, ovens, pet stations, trash disposal, and storage, so that they become, in effect, kitchens within kitchens. Suffice it to say, before you commit to building an island, think long, hard, and diligently about what you want it to do and, no less significantly, how you want it to look. If you get it wrong, there's no getting rid of it. But if your kitchen island is the right one for you, you'll spend almost all your time working with it most gratefully.

There are so many elements here
to admire that it's hard to know
where to begin, though the hanging
glass shelves before the windows
are the obvious starting point.
I love the marble lintel above the
stove, the thick butcher-block
island top, and the brass sink
hardware, each of which combines
sturdy functionality with style. Each
case-goods color serves as a foil
for the other. And the lights above
the island are perfectly scaled.

ABOVE AND OPPOSITE: As these examples suggest, islands—though they remain essentially utilitarian in character—can evince a high degree of elegance. Moreover, if you install more than one, they serve an architectural function by zoning space.

# Surfaces

Choosing the right surfaces is as challenging a task as anything to be found in kitchen design. Like cabinetry and hardware—perhaps to an even greater degree—the walls and countertops you select send a strong stylistic message. At the same time, they have to stand up to the demands of what amounts to a domestic version of an industrial space. What's more, the materials you choose for your kitchen's various planes will in all likelihood be different from each other, and one way or another, they need to interrelate. I would suggest creating a hierarchy of surfaces, beginning with the walls, moving on to the counters and work zones, and concluding with backsplashes. And consider how your surfaces will wear—and the degree to which perfection matters to you. The countertops on which you do most of your chopping may become scratched and stained, which might not be such a bad thing. Would you rather have a pristine surface or one that's a lively record of meals enjoyed and time well spent?

| COUNTERTOP | BACKSPLASH |
|---|---|
| MATERIALS | MATERIALS |
| Natural stone slabs | Marble |
|    Polished |    Slab |
|    Honed |    Dimensional stone |
|    Textured | Onyx |
| Wood or butcher block |    Slab |
| Synthetic slabs |    Dimensional stone |
| Poured concrete | Ceramic tile |
| Stainless steel | Glass tile |
| Terrazzo | Cement tile |
| | Mosaic tesserae |
| | Mosaic waterjet |

The challenge in a kitchen of this scale is to make it feel less imposing. Hence the glass doors in the cabinets, which help to lower the mass of the architecture; light colors to offset the dark-painted wood; and a trio of low-hanging lights to create intimacy.

ABOVE AND OPPOSITE: Given that most of us avoid hanging art in the kitchen (or good art, at any rate), the surfaces we choose stand as the room's dominant decorative component. Tiles bring in color and graphic vitality. Figured stone can be as evocative as an abstract canvas.

# Lighting

A well-known interior designer once observed that after God created the heavens and the earth, "She made dimmer switches." Her quip suggests the absolutely crucial importance of getting the light right in any setting, and the kitchen is no exception. As in the living room or bedroom, your kitchen requires a range of lighting choices, including general illumination, decorative accents, and—most important!—*task lighting*. As in all other rooms in your home, the lights must perform different functions and cohere. Otherwise, you may have a perilous problem of the "Is that chicken done, or is it dark in here?" variety.

| TYPE | FINISHES |
|---|---|
| Pendants | Nickel |
| Recessed task lighting | Brass |
| Flush-mount ceiling lights | Matte nickel |
| Under-counter LEDs | Antique brass |
| Sconces | Chrome |
| Chandeliers | |

Everyone who has ever hung out at a beach bar with unpretentious wicker and wood elements casually assembled knows how enjoyable the experience can be. So why not replicate it with elegance and flair in the kitchen?

# Floors

Kitchen floors matter. Partly because you'll be dropping food and liquids of every sort on them, and they need to be able to take a beating. But floors also matter because, depending on the complexity (or lack thereof) of the rest of the space, they can serve as the room's major decorative element. Floors also set a mood. And depending on whether or not they continue into adjoining spaces, kitchen floors can connect the room to its surroundings or demarcate it as a stand-alone zone. Alas, when it comes to kitchen design, there's no rest for the weary: even the floors demand that we think.

**MATERIALS**

| | |
|---|---|
| Wood | Natural stone |
| Porcelain | Marble |
| Cement tiles | Polished |
| (plain or patterned) | Honed |
| Terra-cotta | Textured |
| Terrazzo | Limestone |
| | Bluestone |
| | Travertine |

Given a sufficiency of space, a kitchen may support a multitude of experiences, for both cooking and dining — and if they can all partake of natural light and a panoramic vista, so much the better.

# Accessories

In my mind, accessories fall into two categories. There are the major ones, notably range goods and pot racks. And then there are the second-tier accessories, for example the aforementioned pot fillers, instant-hot taps, pet-feeding stations, and similar amenities. Consider what small things might make a difference in your kitchen experience. If you hate waiting for the teakettle to start screaming, a tap that dispenses boiling water will put a smile on your face every time it's used.

**TYPE**
Range hood
Pot rack
Instant hot
Garbage disposal
Soap dispenser

If one of the prerequisites of a big, hardworking kitchen is that it should give you an appetite, this one succeeds in spades. Good ideas include the exposed easy-access shelf for tableware, industrial lighting, indestructible work surfaces, and a rug to make things easy on the eyes *and* feet.

# Appliances

The curious paradox regarding kitchen appliances is that they are not precisely a part of kitchen design, yet to many of us, they're the whole story, the stove and refrigerator in particular. It would not be appropriate in this context for me to recommend one brand or another, and in any case I am not equipped to do so. I will opine that it is always advisable to get the best quality you can afford: if a major appliance needs to be replaced, you may find yourself doing a minor renovation. To this, let me add the obvious: think about what you value in a specific appliance, then purchase one that answers your needs. Some of us like automatic ice makers, others find them unnecessary; dedicated chefs might require an extra stove-top burner, which would be wasted on a casual cook. Purchasing appliances is like broiling a steak: don't overdo it, and don't underdo it. Consult your local appliance dealer.

# Practicing What I Preach

My husband, Robert, and I recently moved into a new home after nearly half a century in the previous one, and this afforded us the opportunity to create a kitchen that drew on cherished memories and formative experiences, embraced ideas we'd always wanted to try, corrected functional glitches that had plagued us in our old place, and brought our family's aesthetic into the twenty-first century. At times, designing and building the new kitchen felt akin to writing a novel—and like all well-told tales, this one was constructed out of an immense accretion of detail.

A word to those of you who want to replace a preexisting kitchen, even though—as was the case in our new home—it may be in perfectly good working order. In the past, all of the things you tore out got thrown away, even those that might have enjoyed a second life. But our waste-conscious age has given rise to a welcome alternative: kitchen recycling. There are companies that will remove and cart away all of your old appliances, cabinetry, and surfaces and either resell them or donate to those in need. So if you want to personalize this most personal of all rooms, you can do so in a way that's guilt-free.

And with that, I have run out of advice. Permit me to sign off by offering my own kitchen for your consideration. I hope you find it inspiring, and I wish you the very best of luck in pursuit of the kitchen that's perfect for you.

OPPOSITE: We replaced the single solid door between the kitchen and laundry room with double doors lightened by frosted-glass inserts. The informal dining area adjoins the kitchen and shares its floor-to-ceiling tiles. FOLLOWING PAGES: The narrow island enables us to circulate easily and enjoy the views. Prior to renovation, the sink sat in the rear corner to the left of the stove.

ABOVE: The glass cabinet dematerializes one corner of the kitchen, gives us a place to display favorite objects, and—thanks to hidden rows of tiny LEDs—serves as a night-light.
OPPOSITE: All of the drawers are lined with walnut, delivering both continuity and elegance. The brass handles were selected for how good they feel to the hand and their abstract resemblance to deck cleats, as the house overlooks the boat-filled Long Island Sound.

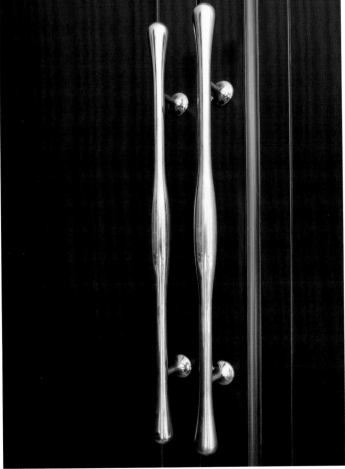

I specified sufficient cabinet space for all of our tableware and glassware. Don't these glasses look extra handsome in their walnut-lined space?

ABOVE AND OPPOSITE: I love convenience, exemplified by the stove's handy pot filler and the dedicated drawer for trash bags directly above the built-in bin. Mesh cabinet fronts lighten the architecture (and can be used to grate potatoes in a pinch). The cabinet handles are a small-scale version of the big ones on the refrigerator doors.

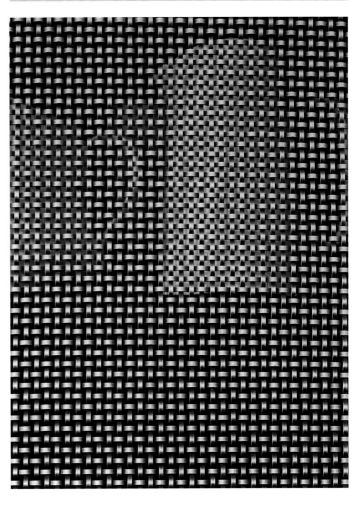

OPPOSITE AND ABOVE: The bar continues the kitchen's decorative motifs while adding a copper sink, a brass faucet, and a marble shelf with brackets made from the same material.

# DESIGN DIRECTORY

# PHOTOGRAPHY CREDITS

Cover, pages 22, 88, 113: Simon Upton

Back cover, pages 5, 6, 20, 26, 32, 33, 42, 43, 47, 96, 97, 99, 130, 139, 154, 179, 185, 190, 206, 219 (top left), 235 (bottom right), 246, 250 (left): Eric Piasecki/OTTO

Endpapers: Henry & Co.

Pages 2, 124, 125, 144, 180, 211, 251: Emily J. Followill Photography

Page 8: Thomas Loof/Art Department

Page 11: American kitchen between 1925 and 1930. Photo via Library of Congress

Page 12: Schlesinger Library, Radcliffe Institute, Harvard University

Page 13: Album/Art Resource, NY

Pages 14, 45, 52, 55, 70, 71, 82, 106, 107, 123, 128, 184, 188, 196, 205, 217 (top left), 242, 250 (right), 257, 258, 260, 261, 262, 264, 265, 266, 267: William Abranowicz/Art + Commerce

Pages 17, 18, 60, 137, 143, 156: Pieter Estersohn/Art Department

Pages 24, 165, 176: Laura Resen

Pages 28, 29, 192: Annie Schlechter

Page 31: Alexander James

Pages 34, 37, 195: Durston Saylor

Pages 36, 229 (bottom right): Noah Webb

Page 38: François Halard/Trunk Archive

Page 40: Max Kim-Bee/OTTO

Pages 44, 189: Aimée Mazzenga

Pages 48, 50, 202, 214 (bottom right): Laura Hull Photography

Pages 51, 56, 78, 162, 186, 187 (top left and top right), 230, 237: Richard Powers Photographer

Pages 59, 241 (top right), 244: Victoria Pearson

Pages 62, 63: David Duncan Livingston

Pages 64, 194, 200: Francesco Lagnese

Page 66: Douglas Friedman/Trunk Archive

Page 68: Steve Freihon/Tungsten LLC

Pages 72, 100, 104, 120, 181, 182, 214 (top left and bottom left): Erica George Dines

Pages 74, 153: Peter Vitale

Pages 76, 217 (bottom left), 226 (bottom right), 231, 243 (top right): Roger Davies/OTTO

Pages 80, 81: Adrian Gaut/Edge Reps

Pages 84, 85: Gordon Beall

Page 86: Elizabeth Felicella

Pages 87, 229 (top right), 247 (left): Paul Costello/OTTO

Pages 90, 91: William Waldron

Pages 92, 93, 217 (top right), 224, 226 (top right), 229 (top left and bottom left), 238, 241 (bottom right), 248: Trevor Tondro/OTTO

Pages 94, 164: Erik Kvalsvik

Page 98: Tim Clarke Design

Pages 102, 103, 187 (bottom left), 203 (top right and bottom right), 216: Oxford Boone

Pages 108, 110, 215, 217 (bottom right), 218, 219 (top right and bottom left), 225, 226 (top left and bottom left), 235 (bottom left), 241 (top left and bottom left): Gentl and Hyers

Page 109: Eric Wolfinger

Pages 114, 134, 158, 170: Eric Laignel

Pages 116, 118, 243 (bottom left): Joshua McHugh

Pages 126, 214 (top right), 234: Tony Soluri

Page 133: Roehner + Ryan

Page 140: Casey Dunn

Pages 146, 212: Lisa Romerein

Page 148: Nikolas Koenig/OTTO

Page 150: Oberto Gili

Page 151: Peter Murdock

Page 152: Kyle Knodell

Pages 160, 187 (bottom right): Costas Picadas/Dlux Creative

Page 166: Peter Aaron/OTTO

Pages 168, 169: Matthew Millman

Page 172: Meghan Beierle-O'Brien

Page 174: Mina Paz-Le Draoulec

Page 175: Edward Acker

Page 183: Stephen Kent Johnson/OTTO

Pages 191, 201: Tria Giovan Photography

Page 193: Michal Venera

Page 198: Jonathan Wallen

Pages 199, 209, 222: The Ingalls

Page 203 (top left): Julie Soefer

Pages 203 (bottom left), 221: Tessa Neustadt

Page 204: Lorin Klaris

Page 219 (bottom right): Ben Robertson

Page 227: Simon Plant

Page 228: ChiChi Ubiña

Pages 232, 255: Belathée Photography

Page 235 (top): James Merrell

Page 240: Zach Lipp

Page 243 (top left): Laurey Glenn

Page 243 (bottom right): David A. Land/OTTO

Page 247 (right): Eric Roth

Page 252: Stephen Karlisch/stephenkarlisch.com

# Acknowledgments

I have poignant childhood memories of my grandmother's kitchen. I recall a very large white porcelain sink with a long drain board and a wall-mounted faucet. There was a huge table in the middle where we sliced, chopped, mixed, and assembled. We were aunts, female cousins, mothers, granddaughters, and grandmother—a sisterhood, a team, a family, a community working in concert before each glorious and food-laden holiday feast. I can still smell the honey cake and roasting chicken.

I hope the occupants of the kitchens pictured in this book are creating similarly enriching and soulful memories of their own. Each of these spaces—large or small; formal or casual; traditional, transitional or modern—represents a wonderful spot to gather and work, to enjoy a glass of wine with friends, to prepare a family dinner or experiment with a new recipe, to do homework or to simply hang out.

Much like creating a kitchen, this book has required a fairly significant and experienced team. I'm so grateful to all the designers and architects who submitted their projects for *The Perfect Kitchen*. My only regret is that we couldn't publish them all.

The dynamo Jill Cohen really gets things done! I've appreciated her encouragement, her thoughtful suggestions, and her industry contacts. Lizzy Hyland knows everything—a walking encyclopedia of images, details, and contacts, she's been key to getting this book over the finish line. Many, many thanks to her and her efficiency.

All meetings with Marc Kristal start with movie reviews. Then we get down to business: discussions about style, design, details, imagery, and imagination. The result is a cohesive narrative that's both inspirational and informative. A good friend and collaborator is essential to creating a good book. Marc is the best.

Doug Turshen has designed countless books and is always up for the challenge of making each one different, with its own personality and cadence. I thank him for working with me and for welcoming my ideas. And a special shout-out to Steve Turner who makes it all real.

While Kathleen Jayes stayed quiet throughout the early stages of *The Perfect Kitchen*, she carries a big stick. Her publishing expertise and guidance ensured that our efforts would result in the best book possible.

The team at Waterworks is always helpful and supportive. Many thanks to Hayley Galasso, Laura Hinkley, and Jennifer Scruby, as well as Linda Robertson, who was here at the beginning. And cheers to our start-up cabinetry team, who, with extraordinary dedication, brought our cabinetry business to life.

Finally, a tribute to my remarkable family: Peter, Dan, Robert, Melanie, Elizabeth, Greer, Skyler, Sam, Annie, and Agnes. They nourish, encourage, and support me while making sure I stay grounded. And a special recognition to Peter Sallick for his vision, strategy, fortitude, and leadership of Waterworks, and for his trust that I will bring this book to life.

---

First published in the United States of America in 2020 by Rizzoli International Publications, Inc.
300 Park Avenue South
New York, NY 10010
www.rizzoliusa.com

Copyright © 2020 Barbara Sallick

Text: Marc Kristal
My Perfect Kitchen texts: Julia Turshen, Melissa Clark, Pascale Le Draoulec, Alfred Portale, Brian McCarthy, Ellie Cullman

Publisher: Charles Miers
Senior Editor: Kathleen Jayes
Design: Doug Turshen with Steve Turner
Production Manager: Colin Hough-Trapp
Managing Editor: Lynn Scrabis

Printed in China

2021 2022 2023 2024 / 10 9 8 7 6

ISBN: 978-0-8478-67912
Library of Congress Control Number: 2019950238

Visit us online:
Facebook.com/RizzoliNewYork
Twitter: @Rizzoli_Books
Instagram.com/RizzoliBooks
Pinterest.com/RizzoliBooks
Youtube.com/user/RizzoliNY
Issuu.com/Rizzoli